PHAEDRA

PHAEDRA

2.00

RACINE'S PHÈDRE
in an English version

by

Robert Lowell

FARRAR, STRAUS AND GIROUX
New York

For Miss Harriet Winslow

PHAEDRA

BACKGROUND OF THE ACTION

The story of Racine's *Phèdre* is a Greek myth. Phaedra, the wife of Theseus, the hero and king of Athens, is the daughter of Minos and Pasiphaë, the rulers of Crete. Pasiphaë coupled with a bull, and bore the Minotaur, half bull and half man, who was slain by Theseus in the maze at Crete. Phaedra falls madly in love with her stepson, Hippolytus. She is rejected by him, and falsely accuses him of trying to assault her. Theseus prays to Poseidon, the sea-god, to destroy Hippolytus; Hippolytus is destroyed. Phaedra confesses and kills herself. *Phèdre* is in some ways a miraculous translation and adaptation of Euripides' *Hippolytos*. Racine quite alters and to my mind even surpasses his wonderful original.

ON TRANSLATING PHÈDRE

Racine's plays are generally and correctly thought to be untranslatable. His syllabic alexandrines do not and cannot exist in English. We cannot reproduce his language, which is refined by the literary artifice of his contemporaries, and given a subtle realism and grandeur by the spoken idiom of Louis the Fourteenth's court. Behind each line is a for us lost knowledge of actors and actresses, the stage and the moment. Other qualities remain: the great conception, the tireless plotting, and perhaps the genius for rhetoric and versification that alone proves that the conception and plotting are honest. Matisse says somewhere that a reproduction requires as much talent for color as the original painting. I have been tormented by the fraudulence of my own heavy touch.

My meter, with important differences, is based on Dryden and Pope. In his heroic plays, Dryden uses an end-stopped couplet, loaded with inversions, heavily alliterated, and varied by short un rhymed lines. My couplet is run on, avoids inversions and alliteration, and loosens its rhythm with shifted accents and occasional extra syllables. I gain in naturalness and lose in compactness and epigrammic resonance. I have tried for an idiomatic and ageless style, but I inevitably echo the English Restoration, both in ways that are proper and in my sometimes unRacinian humor and bombast.

My version is *free,* nevertheless I have used every speech in the original, and almost every line is either translated or paraphrased. Racine is said to have written prose drafts and then versed them. We do not have the prose drafts, but I feel sure that necessities of line rhyme, etc. made for changes of phrasing and even of meaning. In versing Racine, I have taken the same liberty. Here and there, I have put in things that no French classical author would have used. Examples are the Amazon in Theramenes' first speech and the *muck* and *jelly* in Phaedra's second act speech. Such interpolations are rare, however.

No translator has had the gifts or the luck to bring Racine into our culture. It's a pity that Pope and Dryden overlooked Racine's great body of works, close to them, in favor of the inaccessible Homer and Virgil.

Racine's verse has a diamond-edge. He is perhaps the greatest poet in the French language, but he uses a smaller vocabulary than any English poet—beside him Pope and Bridges have a Shakespearean luxuriance. He has few verbally inspired lines, and in this is unlike Baudelaire and even La Fontaine. His poetry is great because of the justness of its rhythm and logic, and the glory of its hard, electric rage. I have translated as a poet, and tried to give my lines a certain dignity, speed, and flare.

ROBERT LOWELL

ACKNOWLEDGMENTS

This translation was originally written for Mr. Eric Bentley and one of his classic theater antholgies. I was helped by innumerable suggestions made by friends and experts: Elizabeth Hardwick, Eric Bentley, Jacques Barzun, Stanley Kunitz, William Alfred, Adrienne Rich, Margaret Guiton, Mary Hivnor, and I. A. Richards.

R. L.

CHARACTERS

THESEUS, *son of Aegeus and King of Athens*

PHAEDRA, *wife of Theseus and daughter of Minos and Pasiphaë*

HIPPOLYTUS, *son of Theseus and Antiope, Queen of the Amazons*

ARICIA, *princess of the royal blood of Athens*

OENONE, *nurse of Phaedra*

THERAMENES, *tutor of Hippolytus*

ISMENE, *friend of Aricia*

PANOPE, *waiting-woman of Phaedra*

Guards

Pronunciation:

Phaedra = Pheédra   Aricia = Arísha
Oenone = Eenónee   Theramenes = Therámeneés
Ismene = Ismeénee   Panope = Pánopeé
Pasiphaë = Pásiphá-ee

ACT 1

SCENE I

Hippolytus, Theramenes

HIPPOLYTUS

No, no, my friend, we're off! Six months have passed
since Father heard the ocean howl and cast
his galley on the Aegean's skull-white froth.
Listen! The blank sea calls us—off, off, off!
I'll follow Father to the fountainhead
and marsh of hell. We're off. Alive or dead,
I'll find him.

THERAMENES

Where, my lord? I've sent a host
of veteran seamen up and down the coast;

each village, creek and cove from here to Crete
has been ransacked and questioned by my fleet;
my flagship skirted Hades' rapids, furled
sail there a day, and scoured the underworld.
Have you fresh news? New hopes? One even doubts
if noble Theseus wants his whereabouts
discovered. Does he need helpers to share
the plunder of his latest love affair;
a shipload of spectators and his son
to watch him ruin his last Amazon—
some creature, taller than a man, whose tanned
and single bosom slithers from his hand,
when he leaps to crush her like a waterfall
of honeysuckle?

HIPPOLYTUS

       You are cynical,
my friend. Your insinuations wrong a king,
sick as myself of his philandering.
His heart is Phaedra's and no rivals dare
to challenge Phaedra's sole possession there.
I sail to find my father. The command
of duty calls me from this stifling land.

THERAMENES

This stifling land? Is that how you deride
this gentle province where you used to ride
the bridle-paths, pursuing happiness?
You cured your orphaned childhood's loneliness
and found a peace here you preferred to all
the blaze of Athens' brawling protocol.
A rage for exploits blinds you. Your disease
is boredom.

HIPPOLYTUS

      Friend, this kingdom lost its peace,
when Father left my mother for defiled
bull-serviced Pasiphaë's child. The child
of homicidal Minos is our queen!

THERAMENES

Yes, Phaedra reigns and rules here. I have seen
you crouch before her outbursts like a cur.
When she first met you, she refused to stir
until your father drove you out of court.
The news is better now; our friends report
the queen is dying. Will you cross the seas,
desert your party and abandon Greece?
Why flee from Phaedra? Phaedra fears the night
less than she fears the day that strives to light
the universal ennui of her eye—
this dying woman, who desires to die!

HIPPOLYTUS

No, I despise her Cretan vanity,
hysteria and idle cruelty.
I fear Aricia; she alone survives
the blood-feud that destroyed her brothers' lives.

THERAMENES

Prince, Prince, forgive my laughter. Must you fly
beyond the limits of the world and die,
floating in flotsam, friendless, far from help,
and clubbed to death by Tartars in the kelp?
Why arm the shrinking violet with a knife?
Do you hate Aricia, and fear for your life,
Prince?

HIPPOLYTUS

    If I hated her, I'd trust myself
and stay.

THERAMENES

    Shall I explain you to yourself?
Prince, you have ceased to be that hard-mouthed, proud
and pure Hippolytus, who scorned the crowd
of common lovers once and rose above
your wayward father by despising love.
Now you justify your father, and you feel
love's poison running through you, now you kneel
and breathe the heavy incense, and a god
possesses you and revels in your blood!
Are you in love?

HIPPOLYTUS

    Theramenes, when I call
and cry for help, you push me to the wall.
Why do you plague me, and try to make me fear
the qualities you taught me to revere?
I sucked in prudence with my mother's milk.
Antiope, no harlot draped in silk,
first hardened me. I was my mother's son
and not my father's. When the Amazon,
my mother, was dethroned, my mind approved
her lessons more than ever. I still loved
her bristling chastity. Later, you told
stories about my father's deeds that made me hold
back judgment—how he stood for Hercules,
a second Hercules who cleared the Cretan seas
of pirates, throttled Scirron, Cercyon,

Procrustes, Sinnis, and the giant man
of Epidaurus writhing in his gore.
He pierced the maze and killed the Minotaur.
Other things turned my stomach: that long list
of women, all refusing to resist.
Helen, caught up with all her honeyed flesh
from Sparta; Periboea, young and fresh,
already tired of Salinis. A hundred more,
their names forgotten by my father—whore
and virgin, child and mother, all deceived,
if their protestations can be believed!
Ariadne declaiming to the rocks,
her sister, Phaedra, kidnapped. Phaedra locks
the gate at last! You know how often I
would weary, fall to nodding and deny
the possibility of hearing the whole
ignoble, dull, insipid boast unroll.
And now I too must fall. The gods have made me creep.
How can I be in love? I have no specious heap
of honors, friend. No mastered monsters drape
my shoulders—Theseus' excuse to rape
at will. Suppose I chose a woman. Why
choose an orphan? Aricia is eternally
cut off from marriage, lest she breed
successors to her fierce brothers, and seed
the land with treason. Father only grants
her life on one condition. This—he wants
no bridal torch to burn for her. Unwooed
and childless, she must answer for the blood
her brothers shed. How can I marry her,
gaily subvert our kingdom's character,
and sail on the high seas of love?

THERAMENES

You'll prove
nothing by reason, for you are in love.
Theseus' injustice to Aricia throws
her in the light; your eyes he wished to close
are open. She dazzles you. Her pitiful
seclusion makes her doubly terrible.
Does this innocent passion freeze your blood?
There's sweetness in it. Is your only good
the dismal famine of your chastity?
You shun your father's path? Where would you be,
Prince, if Antiope had never burned
chastely for Theseus? Love, my lord, has turned
the head of Hercules, and thousands—fired
the forge of Vulcan! All your uninspired,
cold moralizing is nothing, Prince. You have changed!
Now no one sees you riding, half-deranged
along the sand-bars, where you drove your horse
and foaming chariot with all your force,
tilting and staggering upright through the surf—
far from their usual course across the turf.
The woods are quiet . . . How your eyes hang down!
You often murmur and forget to frown.
All's out, Prince. You're in love; you burn. Flames, flames,
Prince! A dissimulated sickness maims
the youthful quickness of your daring. Does
lovely Aricia haunt you?

HIPPOLYTUS

Friend, spare us.
I sail to find my father.

THERAMENES

Will you see
Phaedra before you go?

HIPPOLYTUS

I mean to be
here when she comes. Go, tell her. I will do
my duty. Wait, I see her nurse. What new
troubles torment her?

SCENE II

Hippolytus, Theramenes, Oenone

OENONE

Who has griefs like mine,
my lord? I cannot help the queen in her decline.
Although I sit beside her day and night,
she shuts her eyes and withers in my sight.
An eternal tumult roisters through her head,
panics her sleep, and drags her from her bed.
Just now she fled me at the prime
of day to see the sun for the last time.
She's coming.

HIPPOLYTUS

So! I'll steal away. My flight
removes a hateful object from her sight.

SCENE III

Phaedra, Oenone

PHAEDRA

Dearest, we'll go no further. I must rest.
I'll sit here. My emotions shake my breast,
the sunlight throws black bars across my eyes.
My knees give. If I fall, why should I rise,
Nurse?

OENONE

Heaven help us! Let me comfort you.

PHAEDRA

Tear off these gross, official rings, undo
these royal veils. They drag me to the ground.
Why have you frilled me, laced me, crowned me, and wound
my hair in turrets? All your skill torments
and chokes me. I am crushed by ornaments.
Everything hurts me, and drags me to my knees!

OENONE

Now this, now that, Madam. You never cease
commanding us, then cancelling your commands.
You feel your strength return, summon all hands
to dress you like a bride, then say you choke!
We open all the windows, fetch a cloak,
rush you outdoors. It's no use, you decide
that sunlight kills you, and only want to hide.

PHAEDRA

I feel the heavens' royal radiance cool
and fail, as if it feared my terrible
shame has destroyed its right to shine on men.
I'll never look upon the sun again.

OENONE

Renunciation or renunciation!
Now you slander the source of your creation.
Why do you run to death and tear your hair?

PHAEDRA

Oh God, take me to some sunless forest lair . . .
There hoof-beats raise a dust-cloud, and my eye
follows a horseman outlined on the sky!

OENONE

What's this, my lady?

PHAEDRA

                    I have lost my mind.
Where am I? Oh forget my words! I find
I've lost the habit now of talking sense.
My face is red and guilty—evidence
of treason! I've betrayed my darkest fears,
Nurse, and my eyes, despite me, fill with tears.

OENONE

Lady, if you must weep, weep for your silence
that filled your days and mine with violence.
Ah deaf to argument and numb to care,
you have no mercy. Spare me, spare
yourself. Your blood is like polluted water,

fouling a mind desiring its own slaughter.
The sun has died and shadows filled the skies
thrice now, since you have closed your eyes;
the day has broken through the night's content
thrice now, since you have tasted nourishment.
Is your salvation from your terrified
conscience this passive, servile suicide?
Lady, your madness harms the gods who gave
you life, betrays your husband. Who will save
your children? Your downfall will orphan them,
deprive them of their kingdom, and condemn
their lives and future to the discipline
of one who abhors you and all your kin,
a tyrant suckled by an amazon,
Hippolytus . . .

PHAEDRA

Oh God!

OENONE

You still hate someone;
thank heaven for that, Madam!

PHAEDRA

You spoke his name!

OENONE

Hippolytus, Hippolytus! There's hope
in hatred, Lady. Give your anger rope.
I love your anger. If the winds of love
and fury stir you, you will live. Above
your children towers this foreigner, this child
of Scythian cannibals, now wild

to ruin the kingdom, master Greece, and choke
the children of the gods beneath his yoke.
Why dawdle? Why deliberate at length?
Oh, gather up your dissipated strength.

PHAEDRA

I've lived too long.

OENONE

Always, always agonized!
Is your conscience still stunned and paralyzed?
Do you think you have washed your hands in blood?

PHAEDRA

Thank God, my hands are clean still. Would to God
my heart were innocent!

OENONE

Your heart, your heart!
What have you done that tears your soul apart?

PHAEDRA

I've said too much. Oenone, let me die;
by dying I shall escape blasphemy.

OENONE

Search for another hand to close your eyes.
Oh cruel Queen, I see that you despise
my sorrow and devotion. I'll die first,
and end the anguish of this service cursed
by your perversity. A thousand roads
always lie open to the killing gods.
I'll choose the nearest. Lady, tell me how

Oenone's love has failed you. Will you allow
your nurse to die, your nurse, who gave up all—
nation, parents, children, to serve in thrall.
I saved you from your mother, King Minos' wife!
Will your death pay me for giving up my life?

PHAEDRA

What I could tell you, I have told you. Nurse,
only my silence saves me from the curse
of heaven.

OENONE

How could you tell me anything
worse than watching you dying?

PHAEDRA

I would bring
my life and rank dishonor. What can I say
to save myself, or put off death a day.

OENONE

Ah Lady, I implore you by my tears,
and by your suffering body. Heaven hears,
and knows the truth already. Let me see.

PHAEDRA

Stand up.

OENONE

Your hesitation's killing me!

PHAEDRA

What can I tell you? How the gods reprove
me!

OENONE

Speak!

PHAEDRA

Oh Venus, murdering Venus! love
gored Pasiphaë with the bull.

OENONE

Forget
your mother! When she died, she paid her debt.

PHAEDRA

Oh Ariadne, oh my Sister, lost
for love of Theseus on that rocky coast.

OENONE

Lady, what nervous languor makes you rave
against your family; they are in the grave.

PHAEDRA

Remorseless Aphrodite drives me. I,
my race's last and worst love-victim, die.

OENONE

Are you in love?

PHAEDRA

I am insane with love!

OENONE

Who
is he?

PHAEDRA

    I'll tell you. Nothing love can do
could equal . . . Nurse, I am in love. The shame
kills me. I love the . . . Do not ask his name.

OENONE

Who?

PHAEDRA

    Nurse, you know my old loathing for the son
of Theseus and the barbarous amazon?

OENONE

Hippolytus! My God, oh my God!

PHAEDRA

                        You,
not I, have named him.

OENONE

                What can you do,
but die? Your words have turned my blood to ice.
Oh righteous heavens, must the blasphemies
of Pasiphaë fall upon her daughter?
Her Furies strike us down across the water.
Why did we come here?

PHAEDRA

My evil comes from farther off. In May,
in brilliant Athens, on my marriage day,
I turned aside for shelter from the smile
of Theseus. Death was frowning in an aisle—
Hippolytus! I saw his face, turned white!

My lost and dazzled eyes saw only night,
capricious burnings flickered through my bleak
abandoned flesh. I could not breathe or speak.
I faced my flaming executioner,
Aphrodite, my mother's murderer!
I tried to calm her wrath by flowers and praise,
I built her a temple, fretted months and days
on decoration. I even hoped to find
symbols and stays for my distracted mind,
searching the guts of sacrificial steers.
Yet when my erring passions, mutineers
to virtue, offered incense at the shrine
of love, I failed to silence the malign
Goddess. Alas, my hungry open mouth,
thirsting with adoration, tasted drouth—
Venus resigned her altar to my new lord—
and even while I was praying, I adored
Hippolytus above the sacred flame,
now offered to his name I could not name.
I fled him, yet he stormed me in disguise,
and seemed to watch me from his father's eyes.
I even turned against myself, screwed up
my slack courage to fury, and would not stop
shrieking and raging, till half-dead with love
and the hatred of a stepmother, I drove
Hippolytus in exile from the rest
and strenuous wardship of his father's breast.
Then I could breathe, Oenone; he was gone;
my lazy, nerveless days meandered on
through dreams and daydreams, like a stately carriage
touring the level landscape of my marriage.
Yet nothing worked. My husband sent me here
to Troezen, far from Athens; once again the dear

face shattered me; I saw Hippolytus
each day, and felt my ancient, venomous
passion tear my body limb from limb;
naked Venus was clawing down her victim.
What could I do? Each moment, terrified
by loose diseased emotions, now I cried
for death to save my glory and expel
my gloomy frenzy from this world, my hell.
And yet your tears and words bewildered me,
and so endangered my tranquillity,
at last I spoke. Nurse, I shall not repent,
if you will leave me the passive content
of dry silence and solitude.

SCENE IV

Phaedra, Oenone, Panope

PANOPE

My heart breaks. Would to God, I could refuse
to tell your majesty my evil news.
The King is dead! Listen, the heavens ring
with shouts and lamentations for the King.

PHAEDRA

The King is dead? What's this?

PANOPE

In vain
you beg the gods to send him back again.

Hippolytus has heard the true report,
he is already heading for the port.

PHAEDRA

Oh God!

PANOPE

      They've heard in Athens. Everyone
is joining factions—some salute your son,
others are calling for Hippolytus;
they want him to reform and harden us—
even Aricia claims the loyalty
of a fanatical minority.
The Prince's captains have recalled their men.
His flag is up and now he sails again
for Athens. Queen, if he appear there now,
he'll drag the people with him!

OENONE

          Stop, allow
the Queen a little respite for her grief.
She hears you, and will act for our relief.

SCENE V

Phaedra, Oenone

OENONE

I'd given up persuading you to live;
death was your refuge, only death could give

you peace and save your troubled glory. I
myself desired to follow you, and die.
But this catastrophe prescribes new laws:
the king is dead, and for the king who was,
fate offers you his kingdom. You have a son;
he should be king! If you abandon
him, he'll be a slave. The gods, his ancestors,
will curse and drive you on your fatal course.
Live! Who'll condemn you if you love and woo
the Prince? Your stepson is no kin to you,
now that your royal husband's death has cut
and freed you from the throttling marriage-knot.
Do not torment the Prince with persecution,
and give a leader to the revolution;
no, win his friendship, bind him to your side.
Give him this city and its countryside.
He will renounce the walls of Athens, piled
stone on stone by Minerva for your child.
Stand with Hippolytus, annihilate
Aricia's faction, and possess the state!

PHAEDRA

So be it! Your superior force has won.
I will live if compassion for my son,
devotion to the Prince, and love of power
can give me courage in this fearful hour.

ACT 2

SCENE I

Aricia, Ismene

ARICIA

What's this? The Prince has sent a messenger?
The Prince begs me to wait and meet him here?
The Prince begs! Goose, you've lost your feeble wits!

ISMENE

Lady, be calm. These are the benefits
of Theseus' death: first Prince Hippolytus
comes courting favors; soon the populous
cities of Greece will follow—they will eat
out of your hand, Princess, and kiss your feet.

ARICIA

This felon's hand, this slave's! My dear, your news
is only frivolous gossip, I refuse
to hope.

ISMENE

Ah Princess, the just powers of hell
have struck. Theseus has joined your brothers!

ARICIA

Tell

me how he died.

ISMENE

Princess, fearful tales
are circulating. Sailors saw his sails,
his infamous black sails, spin round and round
in Charybdis' whirlpool; all hands were drowned.
Yet others say on better evidence
that Theseus and Pirithoüs passed the dense
darkness of hell to rape Persephone.
Pirithoüs was murdered by the hound;
Theseus, still living, was buried in the ground.

ARICIA

This is an old wives' tale. Only the dead
enter the underworld, and see the bed
of Queen Persephone. What brought him there?

ISMENE

Princess, the King is dead—dead! Everywhere
men know and mourn. Already our worshipping
townsmen acclaim Hippolytus for their king;

in her great palace, Phaedra, the self-styled
regent, rages and trembles for her child.

ARICIA

What makes you think the puritanical
son of Theseus is human. Will he recall
my sentence and relent?

ISMENE

I know he will.

ARICIA

You know nothing about him. He would kill
a woman, rather than be kind to one.
That wolf-cub of a fighting amazon
hates me above all women. He would walk
from here to hell, rather than hear me talk.

ISMENE

Do you know Hippolytus? Listen to me.
His famous, blasphemous frigidity,
what is it, when you've seen him close at hand?
I've watched him like a hawk, and seen him stand
shaking beside you—all his reputation
for hating womenkind bears no relation
to what I saw. He couldn't take his eyes
off you! His eyes speak what his tongue denies.

ARICIA

I can't believe you. Your story's absurd!
How greedily I listen to each word!
Ismene, you know me, you know how my heart
was reared on death, and always set apart

from what it cherished—can this plaything of
the gods and furies feel the peace of love?
What sights I've seen, Ismene! "Heads will roll,"
my brothers told me, "we will rule." I, the sole
survivor of those fabulous kings, who tilled
the soil of Greece, have seen my brothers killed,
six brothers murdered! In a single hour,
the tyrant, Theseus, lopped them in their flower.
The monster spared my life, and yet decreed
the torments of this childless life I lead
in exile, where no Greek can look on me;
my forced, perpetual virginity
preserves his crown; no son shall bear my name
or blow my brothers' ashes into flame.
Ismene, you know how well his tyranny
favors my temperament and strengthens me
to guard the honor of my reputation;
his rigor fortified my inclination.
How could I test his son's civilities?
I'd never even seen him with my eyes!
I'd never seen him. I'd restrained my eye,
that giddy nerve, from dwelling thoughtlessly
upon his outward grace and beauty—on mere
embellishments of nature, a veneer
the Prince himself despises and ignores.
My heart loves nobler virtues, and adores
in him his father's hard intelligence.
He has his father's daring and a sense
of honor his father lacks. Let me confess,
I love him for his lofty haughtiness
never submitted to a woman's yoke.
How could Phaedra's splendid marriage provoke
my jealousy? Have I so little pride,

I'd snatch at a rake's heart, a heart denied
to none—all riddled, opened up to let
thousands pass in like water through a net?
To carry sorrows to a heart, alone
untouched by passion, inflexible as stone,
to fasten my dominion on a force
as nervous as a never-harnessed horse—
this stirs me, this enflames me. Devilish Zeus
is easier mastered than Hippolytus;
heaven's love-infatuated emperor
confers less glory on his conqueror!
Ismene, I'm afraid. Why should I boast?
His very virtues I admire most
threaten to rise and throw me from the brink
of hope. What girlish folly made me think
Hippolytus could love Aricia?

ISMENE

Here
he is. He loves you, Princess. Have no fear.

SCENE II

Aricia, Ismene, Hippolytus

HIPPOLYTUS

Princess, before
I leave here, I must tell you what's in store
for you in Greece. Alas, my father's dead.
The fierce forebodings that disquieted

my peace are true. Death, only death, could hide
his valor from this world he pacified.
The homicidal Fates will not release
the comrade, friend and peer of Hercules.
Princess, I trust your hate will not resent
honors whose justice is self-evident.
A single hope alleviates my grief,
Princess, I hope to offer you relief.
I now revoke a law whose cruelty
has pained my conscience. Princess, you are free
to marry. Oh enjoy this province, whose
honest, unhesitating subjects choose
Hippolytus for king. Live free as air,
here, free as I am, much more free!

ARICIA

I dare
not hope. You are too gracious. Can you free
Aricia from your father's stern decree?

HIPPOLYTUS

Princess, the Athenian people, torn in two
between myself and Phaedra's son, want you.

ARICIA

Want me, my Lord!

HIPPOLYTUS

I've no illusions. Lame
Athenian precedents condemn my claim,
because my mother was a foreigner.
But what is that? If my only rival were
my younger brother, his minority

would clear my legal disability.
However, a better claim than his or mine
now favors you, ennobled by the line
of great Erectheus. Your direct descent
sets you before my father; he was only lent
this kingdom by adoption. Once the common
Athenian, dazed by Theseus' superhuman
energies, had no longing to exhume
the rights that rushed your brothers to their doom.
Now Athens calls you home; the ancient feud
too long has stained the sacred olive wood;
blood festers in the furrows of our soil
to blight its fruits and scorch the farmer's toil.
This province suits me; let the vines of Crete
offer my brother a secure retreat.
The rest is yours. All Attica is yours;
I go to win you what your right assures.

ARICIA

Am I awake, my lord? Your sayings seem
like weird phantasmagoria in a dream.
How can your sparkling promises be true?
Some god, my lord, some god, has entered you!
How justly you are worshiped in this town;
oh how the truth surpasses your renown!
You wish to endow me with your heritage!
I only hoped you would not hate me. This rage
your father felt, how can you put it by
and treat me kindly?

HIPPOLYTUS

Princess, is my eye
blind to beauty? Am I a bear, a bull, a boar,

some abortion fathered by the Minotaur?
Some one-eyed Cyclops, able to resist
Aricia's loveliness and still exist?
How can a man stand up against your grace?

ARICIA

My lord, my lord!

HIPPOLYTUS
                        I cannot hide my face,
Princess! I'm driven. Why does my violence
so silence reason and intelligence?
Must I be still, and let my adoration
simmer away in silent resignation?
Princess, I've lost all power to restrain
myself. You see a madman, whose insane
pride hated love, and hoped to sit ashore,
watching the galleys founder in the war;
I was Diana's liegeman, dressed in steel.
I hoped to trample love beneath my heel—
alas, the flaming Venus burns me down,
I am the last dependent on her crown.
What left me charred and writhing in her clutch?
A single moment and a single touch.
Six months now, bounding like a wounded stag,
I've tried to shake this poisoned dart, and drag
myself to safety from your eyes that blind
when present, and when absent leave behind
volleys of burning arrows in my mind.
Ah Princess, shall I dive into the sea,
or steal the wings of Icarus to flee
love's Midas' touch that turns my world to gold?
Your image drives me stumbling through the cold,

floods my deserted forest caves with light,
darkens the day and dazzles through my night.
I'm grafted to your side by all I see;
all things unite us and imprison me.
I have no courage for the Spartan exercise
that trained my hand and steeled my energies.
Where are my horses? I forget their names.
My triumphs with my chariot at the games
no longer give me strength to mount a horse.
The ocean drives me shuddering from its shores.
Does such a savage conquest make you blush?
My boorish gestures, headlong cries that rush
at you like formless monsters from the sea?
Ah, Princess, hear me! Your serenity
must pardon the distortions of a weak
and new-born lover, forced by you to speak
love's foreign language, words that snarl and yelp . . .
I never could have spoken without your help.

SCENE III

Aricia, Ismene, Hippolytus, Theramenes

THERAMENES

I announce the Queen. She comes hurriedly,
looking for you.

HIPPOLYTUS

    For me!

THERAMENES

       Don't ask me why;
she insisted. I promised I'd prevail
on you to speak with her before you sail.

HIPPOLYTUS

What can she want to hear? What can I say?

ARICIA

Wait for her, here! You cannot turn away.
Forget her malice. Hating her will serve
no purpose. Wait for her! Her tears deserve
your pity.

HIPPOLYTUS

       You're going, Princess? And I must go
to Athens, far from you. How shall I know
if you accept my love.

ARICIA

       My lord, pursue
your gracious promise. Do what you must do,
make Athens tributary to my rule.
Nothing you offer is unacceptable;
yet this empire, so great, so glorious,
is the least precious of your gifts to us.

SCENE IV

Hippolytus, Theramenes

HIPPOLYTUS

We're ready. Wait, the Queen's here. I need you.
You must interrupt this tedious interview.
Hurry down to the ship, then rush back, pale
and breathless. Say the wind's up and we must sail.

SCENE V

Hippolytus, Oenone, Phaedra

PHAEDRA

He's here! Why does he scowl and look away
from me? What shall I do? What shall I say?

OENONE

Speak for your son, he has no other patron.

PHAEDRA

Why are you so impatient to be gone
from us, my lord? Stay! we will weep together.
Pity my son; he too has lost his father.
My own death's near. Rebellion, sick with wrongs,
now like a sea-beast, lifts its slimey prongs,
its muck, its jelly. You alone now stand

to save the state. Who else can understand
a mother? I forget. You will not hear
me! An enemy deserves no pity. I fear
your anger. Must my son, your brother, Prince,
be punished for his cruel mother's sins?

HIPPOLYTUS

I've no such thoughts.

PHAEDRA

                    I persecuted you
blindly, and now you have good reason to
return my impudence. How could you find
the motivation of this heart and mind
that scourged and tortured you, till you began
to lose the calm composure of a man,
and dwindle to a harsh and sullen boy,
a thing of ice, unable to enjoy
the charms of any civilized resource
except the heavy friendship of your horse,
that whirled you far from women, court and throne,
to course the savage woods for wolves alone?
You have good reason, yet if pain's a measure,
no one has less deserved your stern displeasure.
My lord, no one has more deserved compassion.

HIPPOLYTUS

Lady, I understand a mother's passion,
a mother jealous for her children's rights.
How can she spare a first wife's son? Long nights
of plotting, devious ways of quarrelling—
a madhouse! What else can remarriage bring?

Another would have shown equal hostility,
pushed her advantage more outrageously.

PHAEDRA

My lord, if you had known how far my love
and yearning have exalted me above
this usual weakness . . . Our afflicting kinship
is ending . . .

HIPPOLYTUS

　　　　　Madam, the precious minutes slip
by, I fatigue you. Fight against your fears.
Perhaps Poseidon has listened to our tears,
perhaps your husband's still alive. He hears
us, he is surging home—only a short
day's cruise conceals him, as he scuds for port.

PHAEDRA

That's folly, my lord. Who has twice visited
black Hades and the river of the dead
and returned? No, the poisonous Acheron
never lets go. Theseus drifts on and on,
a gutted galley on that clotted waste—
he woos, he wins Persephone, the chaste . . .
What am I saying? Theseus is not dead.
He lives in you. He speaks, he's taller by a head,
I see him, touch him, and my heart—a reef . . .
Ah Prince, I wander. Love betrays my grief . . .

HIPPOLYTUS

No, no, my father lives. Lady, the blind

furies release him; in your loyal mind,
love's fullness holds him, and he cannot die.

PHAEDRA

I hunger for Theseus. Always in my eye
he wanders, not as he appeared in hell,
lascivious eulogist of any belle
he found there, from the lowest to the Queen;
no, faithful, airy, just a little mean
through virtue, charming all, yet young and new,
as we would paint a god—as I now see you!
Your valiant shyness would have graced his speech,
he would have had your stature, eyes, and reach,
Prince, when he flashed across our Cretan waters,
the loved enslaver of King Minos' daughters.
Where were you? How could he conscript the flower
of Athens' youth against my father's power,
and ignore you? You were too young, they say;
you should have voyaged as a stowaway.
No dawdling bypath would have saved our bull,
when your just vengeance thundered through its skull.
There, light of foot, and certain of your goal,
you would have struck my brother's monstrous soul,
and pierced our maze's slow meanders, led
by Ariadne and her subtle thread.
By Ariadne? Prince, *I* would have fought
for precedence; my every flaming thought,
love-quickened, would have shot you through the dark,
straight as an arrow to your quaking mark.
Could I have waited, panting, perishing,
entrusting your survival to a string,
like Ariadne, when she skulked behind,
there at the portal, to bemuse her mind

among the solemn cloisters of the porch?
No, Phaedra would have snatched your burning torch,
and lunged before you, reeling like a priest
of Dionysus to distract the beast.
I would have reached the final corridor
a lap before you, and killed the Minotaur!
Lost in the labyrinth, and at your side,
would it have mattered, if I lived or died?

HIPPOLYTUS

What are you saying, Madam? You forget
my father is your husband!

PHAEDRA

                    I have let
you see my grief for Theseus! How could I
forget my honor and my majesty,
Prince?

HIPPOLYTUS

        Madam, forgive me! My foolish youth
conjectured hideous untruths from your truth.
I cannot face my insolence. Farewell . . .

PHAEDRA

You monster! You understood me too well!
Why do you hang there, speechless, petrified,
polite! My mind whirls. What have I to hide?
Phaedra in all her madness stands before you.
I love you! Fool, I love you, I adore you!
Do not imagine that my mind approved
my first defection, Prince, or that I loved
your youth light-heartedly, and fed my treason

with cowardly compliance, till I lost my reason.
I wished to hate you, but the gods corrupt
us; though I never suffered their abrupt
seductions, shattering advances, I
too bear their sensual lightnings in my thigh.
I too am dying. I have felt the heat
that drove my mother through the fields of Crete,
the bride of Minos, dying for the full
magnetic April thunders of the bull.
I struggled with my sickness, but I found
no grace or magic to preserve my sound
intelligence and honor from this lust,
plowing my body with its horny thrust.
At first I fled you, and when this fell short
of safety, Prince, I exiled you from court.
Alas, my violence to resist you made
my face inhuman, hateful. I was afraid
to kiss my husband lest I love his son.
I made you fear me (this was easily done);
you loathed me more, I ached for you no less.
Misfortune magnified your loveliness.
I grew so wrung and wasted, men mistook
me for the Sibyl. If you could bear to look
your eyes would tell you. Do you believe my passion
is voluntary? That my obscene confession
is some dark trick, some oily artifice?
I came to beg you not to sacrifice
my son, already uncertain of his life.
Ridiculous, mad embassy, for a wife
who loves her stepson! Prince, I only spoke
about myself! Avenge yourself, invoke
your father; a worse monster threatens you
than any Theseus ever fought and slew.

The wife of Theseus loves Hippolytus!
See, Prince! Look, this monster, ravenous
for her execution, will not flinch.
I want your sword's spasmodic final inch.

OENONE

Madam, put down this weapon. Your distress
attracts the people. Fly these witnesses.
Hurry! Stop kneeling! What a time to pray!

SCENE VI

Theramenes, Hippolytus

THERAMENES

Is this Phaedra, fleeing, or rather dragged away
sobbing? Where is your sword? Who tore
this empty scabbard from your belt?

HIPPOLYTUS

                      No more!
Oh let me get away! I face disaster.
Horrors unnerve me. Help! I cannot master
my terror. Phaedra . . . No, I won't expose
her. No! Something I do not dare disclose . . .

THERAMENES

Our ship is ready, but before you leave,
listen! Prince, what we never would believe
has happened: Athens has voted for your brother.

The citizens have made him king. His mother
is regent.

HIPPOLYTUS

Phaedra is in power!

THERAMENES

An envoy sent from Athens came this hour
to place the scepter in her hands. Her son
is king.

HIPPOLYTUS

Almighty gods, you know this woman!
Is it her spotless virtue you reward?

THERAMENES

I've heard a rumor. Someone swam aboard
a ship off Epirus. He claims the King
is still alive. I've searched. I know the thing
is nonsense.

HIPPOLYTUS

Search! Nothing must be neglected.
If the king's dead, I'll rouse the disaffected
people, crown Aricia, and place our lands,
our people, and our lives in worthy hands.

ACT 3

SCENE I

Phaedra, Oenone

PHAEDRA

Why do my people rush to crown me queen?
Who can even want to see me? They have seen
my downfall. Will their praise deliver me?
Oh bury me at the bottom of the sea!
Nurse, I have said too much! Led on by you,
I've said what no one should have listened to.
He listened. How could he pretend my drift
was hidden? Something held him, and made him shift
his ground . . . He only wanted to depart
and hide, while I was pouring out my heart.
Oh how his blushing multiplied my shame!

Why did you hold me back! You are to blame,
Oenone. But for you, I would have killed
myself. Would he have stood there, iron-willed
and merciless, while I fell upon his sword?
He would have snatched it, held me, and restored
my life. No! No!

OENONE

Control yourself! No peace
comes from surrendering to your disease,
Madam. Oh daughter of the kings of Crete,
why are you weeping and fawning at the feet
of this barbarian, less afraid of fate
than of a woman? You must rule the state.

PHAEDRA

Can I, who have no courage to restrain
the insurrection of my passions, reign?
Will the Athenians trust their sovereignty
to me? Love's despotism is crushing me,
I am ruined.

OENONE

Fly!

PHAEDRA

How can I leave him?

OENONE

Lady, you have already banished him.
Can't you take flight?

PHAEDRA

The time for flight has passed.
He knows me now. I rushed beyond the last

limits of modesty, when I confessed.
Hope was no longer blasting through my breast;
I was resigned to hopelessness and death,
and gasping out my last innocent breath,
Oenone, when you forced me back to life.
You thought I was no longer Theseus' wife,
and let me feel that I was free to love.

OENONE

I would have done anything to remove
your danger. Whether I'm guilty or innocent
is all the same to me. Your punishment
should fall on one who tried to kill you, not
on poor Ocnone. Lady, you must plot
and sacrifice this monster, whose unjust
abhorrence left you dying in the dust.
Oh humble him, undo him, oh despise
him! Lady, you must see him with my eyes.

PHAEDRA

Oenone, he was nourished in the woods;
he is all shyness and ungracious moods
because the forests left him half-inhuman.
He's never heard love spoken by a woman!
We've gone too far. Oenone, we're unwise;
perhaps the young man's silence was surprise.

OENONE

His mother, the amazon, was never moved
by men.

PHAEDRA

The boy exists. She must have loved!

OENONE

He has a sullen hatred for our sex.

PHAEDRA

Oh, all the better; rivals will not vex
my chances. Your advice is out of season;
now you must serve my frenzy, not my reason!
You tell me love has never touched his heart;
we'll look, we'll find an undefended part.
He's turned his bronze prows seaward; look, the wind
already blows like a trumpeter behind
his bulging canvas! The Acropolis
of Athens and its empire shall be his!
Hurry, Oenone, hunt the young man down,
blind him with dazzling visions of the crown.
Go tell him I relinquish my command,
I only want the guidance of his hand.
Let him assume these powers that weary me,
he will instruct my son in sovereignty.
Perhaps he will adopt my son, and be
the son and mother's one divinity!
Oenone, rush to him, use every means
to bend and win him; if he fears the Queen's
too proud, he'll listen to her slave. Plead, groan,
insist, say I am giving him my throne . . .
No, say I'm dying!

SCENE II

Phaedra

PHAEDRA

Implacable Aphrodite, now you see
the depths to which your tireless cruelty
has driven Phaedra—here is my bosom;
every thrust and arrow has struck home!
Oh Goddess, if you hunger for renown,
rise now, and shoot a worthier victim down!
Conquer the barbarous Hippolytus,
who mocks the graces and the power of Venus,
and gazes on your godhead with disgust.
Avenge me, Venus! See, my cause is just,
my cause is yours. Oh bend him to my will! . . .
You're back, Oenone? Does he hate me still?

SCENE III

Phaedra, Oenone

OENONE

Your love is folly, dash it from your soul,
gather your scattered pride and self-control,
Madam! I've seen the royal ship arrive.
Theseus is back, Theseus is still alive!
Thousands of voices thunder from the docks.

People are waving flags and climbing rocks.
While I was looking for Hippolytus . . .

PHAEDRA

My husband's living! Must you trouble us
by talking? What am I living for?
He lives, Oenone, let me hear no more
about it.

OENONE

Why?

PHAEDRA

I told you, but my fears
were stilled, alas, and smothered by your tears.
Had I died this morning, I might have faced
the gods. I heeded you and die disgraced!

OENONE

You are disgraced!

PHAEDRA

Oh Gods of wrath,
how far I've travelled on my dangerous path!
I go to meet my husband; at his side
will stand Hippolytus. How shall I hide
my thick adulterous passion for this youth,
who has rejected me, and knows the truth?
Will the stern Prince stand smiling and approve
the labored histrionics of my love
for Theseus, see my lips, still languishing
for his, betray his father and his King?
Will he not draw his sword and strike me dead?

Suppose he spares me? What if nothing's said?
Am I a gorgon, or Circe, or the infidel
Medea, stifled by the flames of hell,
yet rising like Aphrodite from the sea,
refreshed and radiant with indecency?
Can I kiss Theseus with dissembled poise?
I think each stone and pillar has a voice.
The very dust rises to disabuse
my husband—to defame me and accuse!
Oenone, I want to die. Death will give
me freedom; oh it's nothing not to live;
death to the unhappy's no catastrophe!
I fear the name that must live after me,
and crush my son until the end of time.
Is his inheritance his mother's crime,
his right to curse me, when my pollution stains
the blood of heaven bubbling in his veins?
The day will come, alas, the day will come,
when nothing will be left to save him from
the voices of despair. If he should live
he'll flee his subjects like a fugitive.

OENONE

He has my pity. Who has ever built
firmer foundations to expose her guilt?
But why expose your son? Is your contribution
for his defense to serve the prosecution?
Suppose you kill yourself? The world will say
you fled your outraged husband in dismay.
Could there be stronger evidence and proof
than Phaedra crushed beneath the horse's hoof
of blasphemous self-destruction to convince
the crowds who'll dance attendance on the Prince?

The crowds will mob your children when they hear
their defamation by a foreigner!
Wouldn't you rather see earth bury us?
Tell me, do you still love Hippolytus?

PHAEDRA

I see him as a beast, who'd murder us.

OENONE

Madam, let the positions be reversed!
You fear the Prince; you must accuse him first.
Who'll dare assert your story is untrue,
if all the evidence shall speak for you:
your present grief, your past despair of mind,
the Prince's sword so luckily left behind?
Do you think Theseus will oppose his son's
second exile? He has consented once!

PHAEDRA

How dare I take this murderous, plunging course?

OENONE

I tremble, Lady, I too feel remorse.
If death could rescue you from infamy,
Madam, I too would follow you and die.
Help me by being silent. I will speak
in such a way the King will only seek
a bloodless exile to assert his rights.
A father is still a father when he smites,
You shudder at this evil sacrifice,
but nothing's evil or too high a price
to save your menaced honor from defeat.
Ah Minos, Minos, you defended Crete

by killing young men? Help us! If the cost
for saving Phaedra is a holocaust
of virtue, Minos, you must sanctify
our undertaking, or watch your daughter die.
I see the King.

PHAEDRA

I see Hippolytus!

SCENE IV

Phaedra, Theseus, Hippolytus, Oenone

THESEUS

Fate's heard me, Phaedra, and removed the bar
that kept me from your arms.

PHAEDRA

Theseus, stop where you are!
Your raptures and endearments are profane.
Your arm must never comfort me again.
You have been wronged, the gods who spared your life
have used your absence to disgrace your wife,
unworthy now to please you or come near.
My only refuge is to disappear.

SCENE V

Theseus, Hippolytus

THESEUS

What a strange welcome! This bewilders me.
My son, what's happened?

HIPPOLYTUS

Phaedra holds the key.
Ask Phaedra. If you love me, let me leave
this kingdom. I'm determined to achieve
some action that will show my strength. I fear
Phaedra. I am afraid of living here,

THESEUS

My son, you want to leave me?

HIPPOLYTUS

I never sought
her grace or favor. Your decision brought
her here from Athens. Your desires prevailed
against my judgment, Father, when you sailed
leaving Phaedra and Aricia in my care.
I've done my duty, now I must prepare
for sterner actions, I must test my skill
on monsters far more dangerous to kill
than any wolf or eagle in this wood.
Release me, I too must prove my manhood.
Oh Father, you were hardly half my age,
when herds of giants writhed before your rage—

you were already famous as the scourge
of insolence. Our people saw you purge
the pirates from the shores of Greece and Thrace,
the harmless merchantman was free to race
the winds, and weary Hercules could pause
from slaughter, knowing you upheld his cause.
The world revered you. I am still unknown;
even my mother's deeds surpass my own.
Some tyrants have escaped you; let me meet
with them and throw their bodies at your feet.
I'll drag them from their wolf-holes; if I die,
my death will show I struggled worthily.
Oh, Father, raise me from oblivion;
my deeds shall tell the universe I am your son.

THESEUS

What do I see? Oh gods, what horror drives
my queen and children fleeing for their lives
before me? If so little warmth remains,
oh why did you release me from my chains?
Why am I hated, and so little loved?
I had a friend, just one. His folly moved
me till I aided his conspiracy
to ravish Queen Persephone.
The gods, tormented by our blasphemous
designs, befogged our minds and blinded us—
we invaded Epirus instead of hell.
There a diseased and subtle tyrant fell
upon us as we slept, and while I stood
by, helpless, monsters crazed for human blood
consumed Pirithoüs. I myself was chained
fast in a death-deep dungeon. I remained
six months there, then the gods had pity,

and put me in possession of the city.
I killed the tyrant; now his body feasts
the famished, pampered bellies of his beasts.
At last, I voyaged home, cast anchor, furled
my sails. When I was rushing to my world—
what am I saying? When my heart and soul
were mine again, unable to control
themselves for longing—who receives me? All run
and shun me, as if I were a skeleton.
Now I myself begin to feel the fear
I inspire. I wish I were a prisoner
again or dead. Speak! Phaedra says my home
was outraged. Who betrayed me? Someone come
and tell me. I have fought for Greece. Will Greece,
sustained by Theseus, give my enemies
asylum in my household? Tell me why
I've no avenger? Is my son a spy?
You will not answer. I must know my fate.
Suspicion chokes me, while I hesitate
and stand here pleading. Wait, let no one stir.
Phaedra shall tell me what has troubled her.

SCENE VI

Hippolytus

HIPPOLYTUS

What now? His anger turns my blood to ice.
Will Phaedra, always uncertain, sacrifice
herself? What will she tell the King? How hot

the air's becoming here! I feel the rot
of love seeping like poison through this house.
I feel the pollution. I cannot rouse
my former loyalties. When I try to gather
the necessary strength to face my father,
my mind spins with some dark presentiment . . .
How can such terror touch the innocent?
I LOVE ARICIA! Father, I confess
my treason to you is my happiness!
I LOVE ARICIA! Will this bring you joy,
our love you have no power to destroy?

ACT 4

SCENE I

Theseus, Oenone

THESEUS

What's this, you tell me he dishonors me,
and has assaulted Phaedra's chastity?
Oh heavy fortune, I no longer know
who loves me, who I am, or where I go.
Who has ever seen such disloyalty
after such love? Such sly audacity!
His youth made no impression on her soul,
so he fell back on force to reach his goal!
I recognize this perjured sword; I gave
him this myself to teach him to be brave!
Oh Zeus, are blood-ties no impediment?

Phaedra tried to save him from punishment!
Why did her silence spare this parricide?

OENONE

She hoped to spare a trusting father's pride.
She felt so sickened by your son's attempt,
his hot eyes leering at her with contempt,
she had no wish to live. She read out her will
to me, then lifted up her arm to kill
herself. I struck the sword out of her hand.
Fainting, she babbled the secret she had planned
to bury with her in the grave. My ears
unwillingly interpreted her tears.

THESEUS

Oh traitor! I know why he seemed to blanch
and toss with terror like an aspen branch
when Phaedra saw him. Now I know why he stood
back, then embraced me so coldly he froze my blood.
Was Athens the first stage for his obscene
attentions? Did he dare attack the Queen
before our marriage?

OENONE

                    Remember her disgust
and hate then? She already feared his lust.

THESEUS

And when I sailed, this started up again?

OENONE

I've hidden nothing. Do you want your pain
redoubled? Phaedra calls me. Let me go,
and save her. I have told you what I know.

SCENE II

Theseus, Hippolytus

THESEUS

My son returns! Oh God, reserved and cool,
dressed in a casual freedom that could fool
the sharpest. Is it right his brows should blaze
and dazzle me with virtue's sacred rays?
Are there not signs? Should not ADULTERER
in looping scarlet script be branded there?

HIPPOLYTUS

What cares becloud your kingly countenance,
Father! What is this irritated glance?
Tell me! Are you afraid to trust your son?

THESEUS

How dare you stand here? May the great Zeus stone
me, if I let my fondness and your birth
protect you! Is my strength which rid the earth
of brigands paralysed? Am I so sick
and senile, any coward with a stick
can strike me? Am I a schoolboy's target? Oh God,
am I food for vultures? Some carrion you must prod
and poke to see if it's alive or dead?
Your hands are moist and itching for my bed,
Coward! Wasn't begetting you enough
dishonor to destroy me? Must I snuff
your perjured life, my own son's life, and stain
a thousand glories? Let the gods restrain

my fury! Fly! live hated and alone—
there are places where my name may be unknown.
Go, find them, follow your disastrous star
through filth; if I discover where you are,
I'll add another body to the hill
of vermin I've extinguished by my skill.
Fly from me, let the grieving storm-winds bear
your contagion from me. You corrupt the air.
I call upon Poseidon. Help me, Lord
of Ocean, help your servant! Once my sword
heaped crucified assassins on your shore
and let them burn like beacons. God, you swore
my first request would be fulfilled. My first!
I never made it. Even through the worst
torments of Epirus I held my peace;
no threat or torture brought me to my knees
beseeching favors; even then I knew
some greater project was reserved for you!
Poseidon, now I kneel. Avenge me, dash
my incestuous son against your rocks, and wash
his dishonor from my household; wave on wave
of roaring nothingness shall be his grave.

HIPPOLYTUS

Phaedra accuses me of lawless love!
Phaedra! My heart stops, I can hardly move
my lips and answer. I have no defense,
if you condemn me without evidence.

THESEUS

Oh coward, you were counting on the Queen
to hide your brutal insolence and screen
your outrage with her weakness! You forgot

something. You dropped your sword and spoiled your plot.
You should have kept it. Surely you had time
to kill the only witness to your crime!

HIPPOLYTUS

Why do I stand this, and forbear to clear
away these lies, and let the truth appear?
I could so easily. Where would you be,
if I spoke out? Respect my loyalty,
Father, respect your own intelligence.
Examine me. What am I? My defense
is my whole life. When have I wavered, when
have I pursued the vices of young men?
Father, you have no scaffolding to rig
your charges on. Small crimes precede the big.
Phaedra accused me of attempting rape!
Am I some Proteus, who can change his shape?
Nature despises such disparities.
Vice, like virtue, advances by degrees.
Bred by Antiope to manly arms,
I hate the fever of this lust that warms
the loins and rots the spirit. I was taught
uprightness by Theramenes. I fought
with wolves, tamed horses, gave my soul to sport,
and shunned the joys of women and the court.
I dislike praise, but those who know me best
grant me one virtue—it's that I detest
the very crimes of which I am accused.
How often you yourself have been amused
and puzzled by my love of purity,
pushed to the point of crudeness. By the sea
and in the forests, I have filled my heart
with freedom, far from women.

THESEUS

When this part
was dropped, could only Phaedra violate
the cold abyss of your immaculate
reptilian soul. How could this funeral urn
contain a heart, a living heart, or burn
for any woman but my wife?

HIPPOLYTUS

Ah no!
Father, I too have seen my passions blow
into a tempest. Why should I conceal
my true offense? I feel, Father, I feel
what other young men feel. I love, I love
Aricia. Father, I love the sister of
your worst enemies. I worship her!
I only feel and breathe and live for her!

THESEUS

You love Aricia? God! No, this is meant
to blind my eyes and throw me off the scent.

HIPPOLYTUS

Father, for six months I have done my worst
to kill this passion. You shall be the first
to know . . . You frown still. Nothing can remove
your dark obsession. Father, what will prove
my innocence? I swear by earth and sky,
and nature's solemn, shining majesty. . . .

THESEUS

Oaths and religion are the common cant

of all betrayers. If you wish to taunt
me, find a better prop than blasphemy.

HIPPOLYTUS

All's blasphemy to eyes that cannot see.
Could even Phaedra bear me such ill will?

THESEUS

Phaedra, Phaedra! Name her again, I'll kill
you! My hand's already on my sword.

HIPPOLYTUS

                                Explain
my terms of exile. What do you ordain?

THESEUS

Sail out across the ocean. Everywhere
on earth and under heaven is too near.

HIPPOLYTUS

Who'll take me in? Oh who will pity me,
and give me bread, if you adandon me?

THESEUS

You'll find fitting companions. Look for friends
who honor everything that most offends.
Pimps and jackals who praise adultery
and incest will protect your purity!

HIPPOLYTUS

Adultery! Is it your privilege
to fling this word in my teeth? I've reached the edge
of madness . . . No, I'll say no more. Compare

my breeding with Phaedra's. Think and beware . . .
She had a mother . . . No, I must not speak.

THESEUS

You devil, you'll attack the queen still weak
from your assault. How can you stand and face
your father? Must I drive you from this place
with my own hand. Run off, or I will flog
you with the flat of my sword like a dog!

SCENE III

Theseus

THESEUS

You go to your inevitable fate,
Child—by the river immortals venerate.
Poseidon gave his word. You cannot fly:
death and the gods march on invisibly.
I loved you once; despite your perfidy,
my bowels writhe inside me. Must you die?
Yes; I am in too deep now to draw back.
What son has placed his father on such a rack?
What father groans for such a monstrous birth?
Oh gods, your thunder throws me to the earth.

SCENE IV

Theseus, Phaedra

PHAEDRA

Theseus, I heard the deluge of your voice,
and stand here trembling. If there's time for choice,
hold back your hand, still bloodless; spare your race!
I supplicate you, I kneel here for grace.
Oh, Theseus, Theseus, will you drench the earth
with your own blood? His virtue, youth and birth
cry out for him. Is he already slain
by you for me—spare me this incestuous pain!

THESEUS

Phaedra, my son's blood has not touched my hand;
and yet I'll be avenged. On sea and land,
spirits, the swift of foot, shall track him down.
Poseidon owes me this. Why do you frown?

PHAEDRA

Poseidon owes you this? What have you done
in anger?

THESEUS

What! You wish to help my son?
No, stir my anger, back me to the hilt,
call for blacker colors to paint his guilt.
Lash, strike and drive me on! You cannot guess
the nerve and fury of his wickedness.
Phaedra, he slandered your sincerity,

he told me your accusation was a lie.
He swore he loved Aricia, he wants to wed
Aricia. . . .

PHAEDRA

What, my lord!

THESEUS

That's what he said.
Of course, I scorn his shallow artifice.
Help me, Poseidon, hear me, sacrifice
my son. I seek the altar. Come! Let us both
kneel down and beg the gods to keep their oath.

SCENE V

Phaedra

PHAEDRA

My husband's gone, still rumbling his own name
and fame. He has no inkling of the flame
his words have started. If he hadn't spoken,
I might have . . . I was on my feet, I'd broken
loose from Oenone, and had just begun
to say I know not what to save his son.
Who knows how far I would have gone? Remorse,
longing and anguish shook me with such force,
I might have told the truth and suffered death,
before this revelation stopped my breath:
Hippolytus is not insensible,

only insensible to me! His dull
heart chases shadows. He is glad to rest
upon Aricia's adolescent breast!
Oh thin abstraction! When I saw his firm
repugnance spurn my passion like a worm,
I thought he had some magic to withstand
the lure of any woman in the land,
and now I see a schoolgirl leads the boy,
as simply as her puppy or a toy.
Was I about to perish for this sham,
this panting hypocrite? Perhaps I am
the only woman that he could refuse!

SCENE VI

Phaedra, Oenone

PHAEDRA

Oenone, dearest, have you heard the news?

OENONE

No, I know nothing, but I am afraid.
How can I follow you? You have betrayed
your life and children. What have you revealed,
Madam?

PHAEDRA

       I have a rival in the field,
Oenone.

OENONE

What?

PHAEDRA

Oenone, he's in love—
this howling monster, able to disprove
my beauty, mock my passion, scorn each prayer,
and face me like a tiger in its lair—
he's tamed, the beast is harnessed to a cart;
Aricia's found an entrance to his heart.

OENONE

Aricia?

PHAEDRA

Nurse, my last calamity
has come. This is the bottom of the sea.
All that preceded this had little force—
the flames of lust, the horrors of remorse,
the prim refusal by my grim young master,
were only feeble hints of this disaster.
They love each other! Passion blinded me.
I let them blind me, let them meet and see
each other freely! Was such bounty wrong?
Oenone, you have known this all along,
you must have seen their meetings, watched them sneak
off to their forest, playing hide-and-seek!
Alas, such rendezvous are no offence:
innocent nature smiles of innocence,
for them each natural impulse was allowed,
each day was summer and without a cloud.

Oenone, nature hated me. I fled
its light, as if a price were on my head.
I shut my eyes and hungered for my end.
Death was the only God my vows could bend.
And even while my desolation served
me gall and tears, I knew I was observed;
I never had security or leisure
for honest weeping, but must steal this pleasure.
Oh hideous pomp; a monarch only wears
the robes of majesty to hide her tears!

OENONE

How can their folly help them? They will never
enjoy its fruit.

PHAEDRA

              Ugh, they will love forever—
even while I am talking, they embrace,
they scorn me, they are laughing in my face!
In the teeth of exile, I hear them swear
they will be true forever, everywhere.
Oenone, have pity on my jealous rage;
I'll kill this happiness that jeers at age.
I'll summon Theseus; hate shall answer hate!
I'll drive my husband to annihilate
Aricia—let no trivial punishment,
her instant death, or bloodless banishment . . .
What am I saying? Have I lost my mind?
I am jealous, and call my husband! Bind
me, gag me; I am frothing with desire.
My husband is alive, and I'm on fire!

For whom? Hippolytus. When I have said
his name, blood fills my eyes, my heart stops dead.
Imposture, incest, murder! I have passed
the limits of damnation; now at last,
my lover's lifeblood is my single good.
Nothing else cools my murderous thirst for blood.
Yet I live on! I live, looked down upon
by my progenitor, the sacred sun,
by Zeus, by Europa, by the universe
of gods and stars, my ancestors. They curse
their daughter. Let me die. In the great night
of Hades, I'll find shelter from their sight.
What am I saying? I've no place to turn:
Minos, my father, holds the judge's urn.
The gods have placed damnation in his hands,
the shades in Hades follow his commands.
Will he not shake and curse his fatal star
that brings his daughter trembling to his bar?
His child by Pasiphaë forced to tell
a thousand sins unclassified in hell?
Father, when you interpret what I speak,
I fear your fortitude will be too weak
to hold the urn. I see you fumbling for
new punishments for crimes unknown before.
You'll be your own child's executioner!
You cannot kill me; look, my murderer
is Venus, who destroyed our family;
Father, she has already murdered me.
I killed myself—and what is worse I wasted
my life for pleasures I have never tasted.
My lover flees me still, and my last gasp
is for the fleeting flesh I failed to clasp.

OENONE

Madam, Madam, cast off this groundless terror!
Is love now an unprecedented error?
You love! What then? You love! Accept your fate.
You're not the first to sail into this strait.
Will chaos overturn the earth and Jove,
because a mortal woman is in love?
Such accidents are easy, all too common.
A woman must submit to being woman.
You curse a failure in the source of things.
Venus has feasted on the hearts of kings;
even the gods, man's judges, feel desire,
Zeus learned to live with his adulterous fire.

PHAEDRA

Must I still listen and drink your poisoned breath?
My death's redoubled on the edge of death.
I'd fled Hippolytus and I was free
till your entreaties stabbed and blinded me,
and dragged me howling to the pit of lust.
Oenone, I was learning to be just.
You fed my malice. Attacking the young Prince
was not enough; you clothed him with my sins.
You wished to kill him; he is dying now,
because of you, and Theseus' brutal vow.
You watch my torture; I'm the last ungorged
scrap rotting in this trap your plots have forged.
What binds you to me? Leave me, go, and die,
may your punishment be to terrify
all those who ruin princes by their lies,
hints, acquiescence, filth, and blasphemies—
panders who grease the grooves of inclination,
and lure our willing bodies from salvation.

Go die, go frighten false flatterers, the worst
friends the gods can give to kings they've cursed!

OENONE

I have given all and left all for her service,
almighty gods! I have been paid my price!

ACT 5

SCENE I

Hippolytus, Aricia

ARICIA

Take a stand, speak the truth, if you respect
your father's glory and your life. Protect
yourself! I'm nothing to you. You consent
without a struggle to your banishment.
If you are weary of Aricia, go;
at least do something to prevent the blow
that dooms your honor and existence—both
at a stroke! Your father must recall his oath;
there is time still, but if the truth's concealed,
you offer your accuser a free field.
Speak to your father!

HIPPOLYTUS

              I've already said
what's lawful. Shall I point to his soiled bed,
tell Athens how his marriage was foresworn,
make Theseus curse the day that he was born?
My aching heart recoils. I only want
God and Aricia for my confidants.
See how I love you; love makes me confide
in you this horror I have tried to hide
from my own heart. My faith must not be broken;
forget, if possible, what I have spoken.
Ah Princess, if even a whisper slips
past you, it will perjure your pure lips.
God's justice is committed to the cause
of those who love him, and uphold his laws;
sooner or later, heaven itself will rise
in wrath and punish Phaedra's blasphemies.
I must not. If I rip away her mask,
I'll kill my father. Give me what I ask.
Do this! Then throw away your chains; it's right
for you to follow me, and share my flight.
Fly from this prison; here the vices seethe
and simmer, virtue has no air to breathe.
In the confusion of my exile, none
will even notice that Aricia's gone.
Banished and broken, Princess, I am still
a force in Greece. Your guards obey my will,
powerful intercessors wish us well:
our neighbors, Argos' citadel
is armed, and in Mycenae our allies
will shelter us, if lying Phaedra tries
to hurry us from our paternal throne,

and steal our sacred titles for her son.
The gods are ours, they urge us to attack.
Why do you tremble, falter and hold back?
Your interests drive me to this sacrifice.
While I'm on fire, your blood has changed to ice.
Princess, is exile more than you can face?

ARICIA

Exile with you, my lord? What sweeter place
is under heaven? Standing at your side,
I'd let the universe and heaven slide.
You're my one love, my king, but can I hope
for peace and honor, Prince, if I elope
unmarried? This . . . I wasn't questioning
the decency of flying from the King.
Is he my father? Only an abject
spirit honors tyrants with respect.
You say you love me. Prince, I am afraid.

HIPPOLYTUS

Aricia, you shall never be betrayed;
accept me! Let our love be sanctified,
then flee from your oppressor as my bride.
Bear witness, oh you gods, our love released
by danger, needs no temple or a priest.
It's faith, not ceremonial, that saves.
Here at the city gates, among these graves
the resting places of my ancient line,
there stands a sacred temple and a shrine.
Here, where no mortal ever swore in vain,
here in these shadows, where eternal pain
is ready to engulf the perjurer;
here heaven's scepter quivers to confer

its final sanction; here, my Love, we'll kneel,
and pray the gods to consecrate and seal
our love. Zeus, the father of the world will stand
here as your father and bestow your hand.
Only the pure shall be our witnesses:
Hera, the guarantor of marriages,
Demeter and the virgin Artemis.

ARICIA

The King is coming. Fly. I'll stay and meet
his anger here and cover your retreat.
Hurry. Be off, send me some friend to guide
my timid footsteps, husband, to your side.

SCENE 11

Theseus, Ismene, Aricia

THESEUS

Oh God, illuminate my troubled mind.
Show me the answer I have failed to find.

ARICIA

Go, Ismene, be ready to escape.

SCENE III

Theseus, Aricia

THESEUS

Princess, you are disturbed. You twist your cape
and blush. The Prince was talking to you. Why
is he running?

ARICIA

We've said our last goodbye,
my lord.

THESEUS

I see the beauty of your eyes
moves even my son, and you have gained a prize
no woman hoped for.

ARICIA

He hasn't taken on
your hatred for me, though he is your son.

THESEUS

I follow. I can hear the oaths he swore.
He knelt, he wept. He has done this before
and worse. You are deceived.

ARICIA

Deceived, my lord?

THESEUS

Princess, are you so rich? Can you afford

to hunger for this lover that my queen
rejected? Your betrayer loves my wife.

ARICIA

How can you bear to blacken his pure life?
Is kingship only for the blind and strong,
unable to distinguish right from wrong?
What insolent prerogative obscures
a light that shines in every eye but yours?
You have betrayed him to his enemies.
What more, my lord? Repent your blasphemies.
Are you not fearful lest the gods so loathe
and hate you they will gratify your oath?
Fear God, my lord, fear God. How many times
he grants men's wishes to expose their crimes.

THESEUS

Love blinds you, Princess, and beclouds your reason.
Your outburst cannot cover up his treason.
My trust's in witnesses that cannot lie.
I have seen Phaedra's tears. She tried to die.

ARICIA

Take care, your Highness. What your killing hand
drove all the thieves and reptiles from the land,
you missed one monster, one was left alive,
one . . . No, I must not name her, Sire, or strive
to save your helpless son; he wants to spare
your reputation. Let me go. I dare
not stay here. If I stayed I'd be too weak
to keep my promise. I'd be forced to speak.

SCENE IV

Theseus

THESEUS

What was she saying? I must try to reach
the meaning of her interrupted speech.
Is it a pitfall? A conspiracy?
Are they plotting together to torture me?
Why did I let the rash, wild girl depart?
What is this whisper crying in my heart?
A secret pity fills my soul with pain.
I must question Oenone once again.
My guards, summon Oenone to the throne.
Quick, bring her. I must talk with her alone.

SCENE V

Theseus, Panope

PANOPE

The Queen's deranged, your Highness. Some accursed
madness is driving her; some fury stalks
behind her back, possesses her, and talks
its evil through her, and blasphemes the world.
She cursed Oenone. Now Oenone's hurled
herself into the ocean, Sire, and drowned.
Why did she do it. No reason can be found.

THESEUS

Oenone's drowned?

PANOPE

Her death has brought no peace.
The cries of Phaedra's troubled soul increase.
Now driven by some sinister unrest,
she snatches up her children to her breast,
pets them and weeps, till something makes her scoff
at her affection, and she drives them off.
Her glance is drunken and irregular,
she looks through us and wonders who we are;
thrice she has started letters to you, Sire,
thrice tossed the shredded fragments in the fire.
Oh call her to you. Help her!

THESEUS

The nurse is drowned? Phaedra wishes to die?
Oh gods! Summon my son. Let him defend
himself, tell him I'm ready to attend.
I want him!

Exit Panope

Neptune, hear me, spare my son!
My vengeance was too hastily begun.
Oh why was I so eager to believe
Oenone's accusation? The gods deceive
the victims they are ready to destroy!

SCENE VI

Theseus, Theramenes

THESEUS

Here is Theramenes. Where is my boy,
my first-born? He was yours to guard and keep.
Where is he? Answer me. What's this? You weep?

THERAMENES

Oh, tardy, futile grief, his blood is shed.
My lord, your son, Hippolytus, is dead.

THESEUS

Oh gods, have mercy!

THERAMENES

                    I saw him die. The most
lovely and innocent of men is lost.

THESEUS

He's dead? The gods have hurried him away
and killed him? . . . just as I began to pray . . .
What sudden thunderbolt has struck him down?

THERAMENES

We'd started out, and hardly left the town.
He held the reins; a few feet to his rear,
a single, silent guard held up a spear.
He followed the Mycenae highroad, deep
in thought, reins dangling, as if half asleep;

his famous horses, only he could hold,
trudged on with lowered heads, and sometimes rolled
their dull eyes slowly—they seemed to have caught
their master's melancholy, and aped his thought.
Then all at once winds struck us like a fist,
we heard a sudden roaring through the mist;
from underground a voice in agony
answered the prolonged groaning of the sea.
We shook, the horses' manes rose on their heads,
and now against a sky of blacks and reds,
we saw the flat waves hump into a mountain
of green-white water rising like a fountain,
as it reached land and crashed with a last roar
to shatter like a galley on the shore.
Out of its fragments rose a monster, half
dragon, half bull; a mouth that seemed to laugh
drooled venom on its dirty yellow scales
and python belly, forking to three tails.
The shore was shaken like a tuning fork,
ships bounced on the stung sea like bits of cork,
the earth moved, and the sun spun round and round,
a sulphur-colored venom swept the ground.
We fled; each felt his useless courage falter,
and sought asylum at a nearby altar.
Only the Prince remained; he wheeled about,
and hurled a javelin through the monster's snout.
Each kept advancing. Flung from the Prince's arm,
dart after dart struck where the blood was warm.
The monster in its death-throes felt defeat,
and bounded howling to the horses' feet.
There its stretched gullet and its armor broke,
and drenched the chariot with blood and smoke,
and then the horses, terror-struck, stampeded.

Their master's whip and shouting went unheeded,
they dragged his breathless body to the spray.
Their red mouths bit the bloody surf, men say
Poseidon stood beside them, that the god
was stabbing at their bellies with a goad.
Their terror drove them crashing on a cliff,
the chariot crashed in two, they ran as if
the Furies screamed and crackled in their manes,
their fallen hero tangled in the reins,
jounced on the rocks behind them. The sweet light
of heaven never will expunge this sight:
the horses that Hippolytus had tamed,
now dragged him headlong, and their mad hooves maimed
his face past recognition. When he tried
to call them, calling only terrified;
faster and ever faster moved their feet,
his body was a piece of bloody meat.
The cliffs and ocean trembled to our shout,
at last their panic failed, they turned about,
and stopped not far from where those hallowed graves,
the Prince's fathers, overlook the waves.
I ran on breathless, guards were at my back,
my master's blood had left a generous track.
The stones were red, each thistle in the mud
was stuck with bits of hair and skin and blood.
I came upon him, called; he stretched his right
hand to me, blinked his eyes, then closed them tight.
"I die," he whispered, "it's the gods' desire.
Friend, stand between Aricia and my sire—
some day enlightened, softened, disabused,
he will lament his son, falsely accused;
then when at last he wishes to appease
my soul, he'll treat my lover well, release

and honor Aricia. . . ." On this word, he died.
Only a broken body testified
he'd lived and loved once. On the sand now lies
something his father will not recognize.

THESEUS

My son, my son! Alas, I stand alone
before the gods. I never can atone.

THERAMENES

Meanwhile Aricia, rushing down the path,
approached us. She was fleeing from your wrath,
my lord, and wished to make Hippolytus
her husband in God's eyes. Then nearing us,
she saw the signs of struggle in the waste,
she saw (oh what a sight) her love defaced,
her young love lying lifeless on the sand.
At first she hardly seemed to understand;
while staring at the body in the grass,
she kept on asking where her lover was.
At last the black and fearful truth broke through
her desolation! She seemed to curse the blue
and murdering ocean, as she caught his head
up in her lap; then fainting lay half dead,
until Ismene somehow summoned back her breath,
restored the child to life—or rather death.
I come, great King, to urge my final task,
your dying son's last outcry was to ask
mercy for poor Aricia, for his bride.
Now Phaedra comes. She killed him. She has lied.

SCENE VII

Theseus, Phaedra, Panope

THESEUS

Ah Phaedra, you have won. He's dead. A man
was killed. Were you watching? His horses ran
him down, and tore his body limb from limb.
Poseidon struck him, Theseus murdered him.
I served you! Tell me why Oenone died?
Was it to save you? Is her suicide
A proof of your truth? No, since he's dead, I must
accept your evidence, just or unjust.
I must believe my faith has been abused;
you have accused him; he shall stand accused.
He's friendless even in the world below.
There the shades fear him! Am I forced to know
the truth? Truth cannot bring my son to life.
If fathers murder, shall I kill my wife
too? Leave me, Phaedra. Far from you, exiled
from Greece, I will lament my murdered child.
I am a murdered gladiator, whirled
in black circles. I want to leave the world;
my whole life rises to increase my guilt—
all those dazzled, dazzling eyes, my glory built
on killing killers. Less known, less magnified,
I might escape, and find a place to hide.
Stand back, Poseidon. I know the gods are hard
to please. I pleased you. This is my reward:
I killed my son. I killed him! Only a god
spares enemies, and wants his servants' blood!

PHAEDRA

No, Theseus, I must disobey your prayer.
Listen to me. I'm dying. I declare
Hippolytus was innocent.

THESEUS

Ah Phaedra, on your evidence, I sent
him to his death. Do you ask me to forgive
my son's assassin? Can I let you live?

PHAEDRA

My time's too short, your highness. It was I,
who lusted for your son with my hot eye.
The flames of Aphrodite maddened me;
I loathed myself, and yearned outrageously
like a starved wolf to fall upon the sheep.
I wished to hold him to me in my sleep
and dreamt I had him. Then Oenone's tears,
troubled my mind; she played upon my fears,
until her pleading forced me to declare
I loved your son. He scorned me. In despair,
I plotted with my nurse, and our conspiracy
made you believe your son assaulted me.
Oenone's punished; fleeing from my wrath,
she drowned herself, and found a too easy path
to death and hell. Perhaps you wonder why
I still survive her, and refuse to die?
Theseus, I stand before you to absolve
your noble son. Sire, only this resolve
upheld me, and made me throw down my knife.
I've chosen a slower way to end my life—
Medea's poison; chills already dart
along my boiling veins and squeeze my heart.

A cold composure I have never known
gives me a moment's poise. I stand alone
and seem to see my outraged husband fade
and waver into death's dissolving shade.
My eyes at last give up their light, and see
the day they've soiled resume its purity.

PANOPE

She's dead, my lord.

THESEUS

                        Would God, all memory
of her and me had died with her! Now I
must live. This knowledge that has come too late
must give me strength and help me expiate
my sacrilegious vow. Let's go, I'll pay
my son the honors he has earned today.
His father's tears shall mingle with his blood.
My love that did my son so little good
asks mercy from his spirit. I declare
Aricia is my daughter and my heir.